Printed By CreateSpace, An Amazon Company

Made in the USA
Columbia, SC
05 August 2020

15622714R00074